THE DRY STONE WALL HANDBOOK

A complete guide to all aspects of building stone walls for farm or garden. Provides clear, practical instructions with sections on laying gravel and cobble paths, costs, tools, safety and the law.

THE
DRY STONE WALL
HANDBOOK

Employing the Permanence and Beauty
of Natural Stone

by
Edward Hart

THORSONS PUBLISHERS LIMITED
Wellingborough, Northamptonshire

First published 1980

ISBN 0 7225 0549 3 (paperback)
ISBN 0 7225 0550 7 (hardback)

Photoset by Harper Phototypesetters, Northampton
and printed in Great Britain by
Weatherby Woolnough, Wellingborough, Northamptonshire
on paper made from 100% re-cycled fibre supplied by
P.F. Bingham Limited, Croydon, Surrey

CONTENTS

Chapter   *Page*

 1. Advantages and Drawbacks   9
 2. History and Costs   19
 3. Tools   25
 4. Building the Wall   34
 5. Gates and Stiles   50
 6. Retaining Walls   59
 7. Gravel, Cobbles and Slate   60
 8. Stone in the Garden   66
 9. Flora and Fauna   70
10. Safety and the Law   73
11. Professional Walling, Training and Competitions   79
    Glossary   85
    Bibliography   93
    List of Useful Addresses   94
    Index   95

ACKNOWLEDGEMENTS

Two people have been particularly helpful to me in compiling this book. They are Miss Elizabeth Audland, Secretary of the Dry Stone Walling Association, who has been a source of information and suggestions, and Mr Eric Boyes, a self-employed dyker (waller) who takes care of the vast mileage of walls on the Buccleuch Estates in Dumfriesshire and is one of a long line of dykers who plies his craft with single-minded dedication. I hope some of his infectious enthusiasm comes through on these pages.

Others whose help is acknowledged include Mr J. M. Dent, Mr Ian Dewar of The Agricultural Training Board, Scottish Office; The City of Edinburgh Central Library; The Gladstone Court Museum, Biggar, Lanarkshire; Major W. A. J. Prevost; Mr Denys Tuthill; Mrs Rainsford-Hannay for permission to quote from her late husband's book *Dry Stone Walling;* Gillian Scott for typing the manuscript, and Audrey Hart for photographs and for compiling the index.

AUTHOR'S NOTE

Walls and dykes are synonymous terms where dry stone is concerned. In Scotland a wall is termed a dyke, whereas south of the Border a dyke means a ditch. To avoid constant and tedious repetition of the alternatives, the terms 'wall' and 'waller' are generally used in this book. I hope that Scottish dyking friends will accept my reasons.

1
ADVANTAGES AND DRAWBACKS

Stone is available in abundance over much of the globe. Even in the heart of a city it can be found on derelict sites, and in far flung hill districts its abundance may even be an embarrassment. No material is better suited to the needs of the self-sufficiency enthusiast, and any garden can be enriched in appearance by the proper use of stone.

Though stone walling is an art, it may be learnt by following a few simple rules. The beginner can never hope to match the professional for speed of operation, but after building a very few yards of wall a certain competence is reached. Above all, do not be deluded into a belief that stone walling is a mystique granted only to those born within sight of Snowdonia, Cairngorm or The Cheviot!

A dry stone wall is one built without any additional materials whatever. It is composed simply of natural stone picked up from the field, or quarried without further dressing. No mortar is used although, in certain circumstances, it may be desirable to cement a few stones into place.

Cobble stones and paving flags are other materials that instantly add decades of character to an otherwise raw site. They are decorative, serviceable and readily maintained. Though well built or laid stones should require no maintenance for many years, the ravages of storm or stock must be considered.

The 'March' Walls
Some of the finest walls were built as boundary or 'march' walls between the great estates. They were erected in times when highly skilled labour was both cheap and plentiful. The men who built them were content to toil for twelve hours a day, and perhaps six days a week, living on plain food and with few amenities.

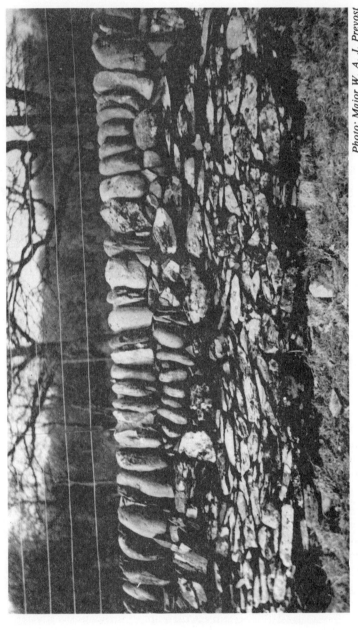

A 'march' dyke round the grounds of 'Caledon' near Gatehouses. Topped in 1978 by Nigel Nicol.

Photo: *Major W. A. J. Prevost*

Therein lies the one great disadvantage of stone walls for the employer. They require as much labour both in making and maintenance as a hundred or two hundred years ago. They cannot be mechanized. Yet to the smallholder or gardener, these factors do not count. Stone walling is a task to be fitted in at any slack season of the year, and there is no cost for materials for repairs. If a piece of wall falls down, the same stones suffice to make it stockproof once more.

The dry stone wall makes an ideal wind-break. It is far more effective than a solid barrier such as a brick or cemented wall which sets up turbulence on its lee side. The dry wall allows air to filter through, at the same time drying stock sheltering in its lee. Thousands of upland lambs are saved by the shelter of dry stone walls when April and May winds cut across the open hills.

Even the most careless picnicker has yet to devise a means of setting fire to a stone wall. This is important in an era when more and more who know nothing about the countryside are so keen to visit it.

It is always an advantage to be able to use home-produced materials. There is no need to import building stone, and most large gardens or small farms either have a supply or can obtain it in the locality.

Haulage is a major factor in the cost of bought stone. For this reason it is pointless to list here the various types of stone because the choice will depend on the stone found in the locality. A Kent householder might import Lakeland stone to make a fireplace of marvellously grained green; he is, however, very unlikely to do so for a length of field or garden wall.

Undoubtedly some districts are more favoured than others. The roadside walls the length of Wensleydale, Yorkshire, are a source of admiration for countless visitors each summer; all due to good workmanship combined with a class of materials which is readily shaped to give an even finish. A few miles away at Masham, there are round, smooth stones like those on a seashore and very difficult indeed to build into a satisfactory barrier. Upland arable districts like the Cotswolds often have flaky pieces of stone which lend their distinctive charm to the walls of the area. In other parts, notably Lakeland, huge, solid rocks are incorporated into the field divisions.

Not only may a dry stone wall be built up an almost sheer face, but the same technique can be used across the hill, to build terraces. These combine function with attractiveness, bringing into use banks so steep

Miles of wall over the Yorkshire uplands.

Stone 'led' off during land reclamation can be used to raise and rebuild this boundary wall.

that they could not possibly be cropped without retaining walls. The vineyards of the Rhine valley are among the better known examples.

Where solid rock lies near the surface, it is impossible to fence with stakes and wire, simply because the stakes cannot be driven into the ground. On such land, the top sod is removed, and beneath is an ideal base for a dry stone wall. Walls are also built across soft land where wooden stakes are likely to rot or cannot be made fast because of the water. However, without solid foundations the wall may be liable to sink.

A stile or gate causes complications with a wire fence. The stone wall simply takes them in its stride; gateways require more square stones than the rest of the wall, but otherwise present no difficulty. A variety of stile designs may be incorporated without weakening the structure, and there is no problem in making them stockproof.

Another purpose of the wall is to use up stones that would otherwise damage field implements. The stoniness of the soil may often be gauged by the size of the fields, the tiny enclosures of the limestone districts around Malham, Yorkshire, being built by rock led from the land surface in years gone by. In some areas, 'consumption' dykes have been built primarily to take the cleared stones.

Although a careful person can climb over a well-built wall without damaging it, use of stiles or gates is infinitely preferable, and rough treatment or an ill-chosen place results in damage. The coping stones (see glossary) may be dislodged, and one Lakeland farmer reported that instructors from an outdoor school actually had a race down the mountainside, knocking tops off walls as they went!

Few tools are needed to build a serviceable wall. Basic equipment includes a spade or shovel for foundations, a medium-weight hammer for splitting the stone, a wooden frame, a steel rule and a length of line (see Chapter 3).

Threats and Drawbacks

A stone wall on a roadside is now a target for thieves. This is especially true near picnic areas where townspeople are wont to gather at weekends. They see a row of nice, even stones set at a convenient height for the car boot and so decide to steal them for the rockery at home. To avoid loss in this way it is necessary to cement in the top course. Single stones, set near a gatepost on a Weardale, County Durham, roadside field were removed several times during the course of one summer, their square shape presenting just too much of a temptation.

Another modern threat to stone walls is the heavy lorry. Down Hartside Pass, in the Lake District, are walls which had stood for decades, until the advent of the motor coach, taking its occupants on sight-seeing expeditions along narrow Lakeland lanes. These lanes, ample for a horse and cart, are little wider than the bus, whose heavy wheels run right up to the wall foundations and unsettle them.

Perhaps the biggest drawback to a stone wall is the time taken to build it. Lifting one stone on top of another takes just as long as it did when men first developed the craft. Some attempts have been made to mix a hopper full of stones and mortar, and tip the lot into a gap, but that cannot be regarded as the answer.

One man's limit per day of a 4½ ft (1.37 m) high wall is only about six or seven yards. The materials has to be carted to him in the first place, no easy task on a steep slope or when remote from supply. A surprisingly large weight of stone is needed; a horse-and-cart load builds only half a yard of wall. Yet the wall lasts many times as long as a fence.

On a fine day, the job is a joy. On a wet or windy one, it is hard graft, and the professional waller cannot afford to pick and choose when he works. Gaps are often mended when the weather is unsuitable for other work, so the idyllic aspect of walling happens more in imagination than fact. The small farmer or gardener can, however, usually choose his time, and build a wall when the sun shines.

If a wall is built too close to a tree, or the tree springs up against the wall, damage may result from root growth. Low-hanging branches are a further hazard when they swing in the wind. The solution is to use a saw and axe.

A pack of hounds is liable to dislodge top stones as they grip with their claws in full cry, but the hunting occupier willingly accepts such slight inconvenience.

Livestock are a continuing menace to the wall's endurance. Some horses are especially damaging. When a horse has filled its belly, it does not lie down to cud like a cow, but wanders in search of mischief. Cows, and especially young heifers, will push at a wall, with its tempting row of coping stones at nose height. A strand of wire is sometimes added to keep stock at bay.

Ewe, lamb and dog are posed unwittingly beside a length of sound wall (right), a potential gap, stones from which have already fallen (centre), and a gap 'cobbled up' as an emergency job (left).

Herdwick sheep under a Lakeland wall. Stakes topped with wire are sometimes needed to make lower walls stockproof. If so the wire should be taut, and not slack as here.

New shepherding methods pose a threat to stone walls. Improved handling facilities, disease prevention and better shearing machines enable one man to look after more sheep. But he cannot repair or build stone walls any faster than did his grandfather, and he now works fewer hours in the week. So there are more sheep per shepherd, but less time in which to maintain walls.

Fortunately, despite these drawbacks, walls continue to be built. The waller's life is more interesting than most. It never becomes routine or mechanical. Every piece of rock is a fresh challenge, to be set so that it bears onto its fellows while remaining in line. The noise and monotony of the factory is entirely absent.

At one time is was feared that the art of walling would die out. This has proved not to be the case, thanks to the efforts of bodies like the Stewartry of Kirkcudbrightshire Drystane Dyking Committee and the Agricultural Training Board. Young Farmers' Clubs have also included walling classes in their show schedules, and this has stimulated interest.

Today prospects for the waller have never been so good; county councils need new walls alongside road widening and improvement schemes, while a housing estate gains immeasurably in character through a few strategically sited walls.

Well-built walls round any garden or farm add to its capital value. As labour becomes increasingly dear, so the value of stone walls will rise.

2
HISTORY AND COSTS

Earliest man built dry stone walls. They do not bear a close resemblance to the Galloway dyke of more recent years, but some notable dry stone constructions remain which were built in the second, third and fourth centuries in the Shetland Islands to give shelter against Danish pirates.

Nearer our own times, farm and croft walls were built around the homesteads, many dating from the fifteenth and sixteenth centuries. Where homesteads were sited in villages, and every villager had a piece of land, some overcrowding was inevitable, and the fields abutting such places were small. Someone would wall in a small garth or enclosure, and then his neighbour secured the adjoining strip, naturally by taking the shortest and easiest practical route. The result is the patchwork effect seen in the Yorkshire dales, where across the valley one can read the story of the intakes, and often see why the small fields have such odd shapes.

In the lowlands, enclosures were naturally of thorn hedge or some other form of wood. It is on the hillsides, upland farms and villages where stone walls are found in such abundance.

Such fields were made from open hill, or waste as it was then termed. The Enclosure Acts bit deeply into these wastes, robbing the independent smallholder of his bit of land and making him totally dependent on another for wages. Thus the stone walls of the late eighteenth and early nineteenth centuries were rooted in ill-feeling.

From 1780 to 1820, the enclosures proceeded, and many of the straight walls over the moors date from that time. In some districts the hillside fields are termed 'allotments', having been allotted to each farmer according to his rights on the upland grazing. Such allotments are a far cry from the suburban patch of that name. They are

Photo: Major W. A. J. Prevost

A sheep fold in Wigtown built of very large single stones.

Photo: Major W. A. J. Prevost

A perfect example of a five-foot high single dyke in Kirkcudbrightshire.

invaluable for tupping and lambing, and other operations when the hill farmer requires rather more control over his flock.

Stone walling is associated with greater production and better agriculture. Its history is part of the story of land reclamation. The Monymusk Consumption Dyke is 5½ feet (1.68 m) high and 27 feet (8.23 m) wide across the top. It was built chiefly to 'consume' the vast amount of stone lying about neighbouring fields. Along its top is a flagged pathway, in smooth contrast to the rough walking on either side.

The ancient dry-built circular castles probably housed the first farmers in Scotland 2,000 years ago. The broch of Nybster at Summerbank, on the north-east coast of Caithness, is but one of many that, according to Geoffrey Grigson in *The Shell Country Alphabet,* 'were built and lived-in between about 100 BC and AD 100 by farming and fishing people of the Iron Age who found themselves in need of tower homesteads or fortified homesteads and by British immigrants who had moved up from the eastern lowlands and Northumberland under pressure from Belgic invaders farther south in Britain. Centuries later their tower houses were named brochs (from Old Norse *borg,* a fort) by Viking settlers or travellers.'

CORNISH STONE HEDGES
by
Denys Tuthill

In Cornwall, a wall is a hedge. Talk to a Cornishman about a wall and he will think of bricks and mortar. A hedge in this county is a construction of stone from the district. They may be built out of granite, elvin, slate, mine waste and are filled with earth and small stones. They are usually topped with turves or 'tobs'. Big spaces between the stones are filled with pieces of turf and eventually the 'hedge' becomes a bulwark of stone, earth, vegetation and roots, which will effectively resist the heavy-weight attentions of bovine inhabitants.

The type of stone used in the hedges varies from district to district. In the West of Cornwall the hedges are constructed chiefly of granite, from Camborne up to Bodmin they are mostly made of brown, flat

Photo: D. E. Tuthill

A fine 'hedge' of dressed granite in Cornwall.

slate stone and in the North around Newquay, Wadebridge, Delabole, a grey slate is used. But there is a type of hedge that was built around estates where deer roamed, which has almost a reverse batter and this was most effective in preventing the deer from leaping onto and over the hedge.

Stone hedges are unique to Cornwall, and date from about the time when the Enclosure Act came into being in about 1700. Before that field boundaries were dry stone walls, but then a shortage of stone demanded that earth be used as a filling.

The craftsmen of today build their hedges to a more definite specification and profile, with the correct 'batter' or slope back, the centre packed with earth and small stones, and the 'cope' or top capped with 'tobs' or grass turves.

Cornwall has numerous dry stone walls, chiefly in the west of the county, and these are quite distinct from the Cornish hedges. Some of the walls are very lovely and in a really fine state of preservation, although over 200 years old. These walls are double-sided, with the centre packed with small pieces of granite. They rise perpendicularly from 4-7 feet (1-2 m), and are so wide that two or three people can walk the top abreast.

Further details may be obtained from the Cornish Stone Hedging Association (see Useful Addresses).

Building Costs

It is impossible to give precise costs of erecting a new dry stone wall, as price of stone varies so much from district to district, and according to the length of haul. The only feasible way is to assess a sum for labour, and another price for the stone.

Before World War I a waller made about 1s. 3d. (6p) per yard, and expected to build a rood a day (the rood being six or seven yards according to the district and type of stone). By World War II, labour costs had approximately tripled.

To build a yard of 4½ feet (1.37 m) wall in 1976 cost about £6 for labour, including digging foundations, setting out and clearing up. Stone and haulage cost a further £13, making a total of £19 per yard.

On that basis, annual costs per yard over 100 years are labour, 6p, stone and haulage, 13p, total 19p per yard.

Allowing for erecting a wire fence seven times in 100 years, the cost over that period is estimated at 8p per yard. This takes no account of inflation, and if stone is already available to hand, the wall may be cheaper over the 100 years period.

Its building, like planting an oak tree, is partly an act of faith. As West Riding farmer Mr J. B. Liddle said to his walling contractor: 'That wall will still be here when I've gone and you've gone!' Meanwhile, its colour, character and shelter add to the beauty of the hillside.

Before 1939 Thomas Firbank bought Dyffryn, a Snowdonia farm of vast elevations and acreage, with extremes of weather to match. In *I Bought a Mountain* he mentioned the comparative costs of walling:

About 1,500 feet up we came upon a high dry stone wall. The wall climbed vertically from the lakes, then turned at right angles to follow the contour of the Glyders, until it swung downhill again to join the road far up the valley. It formed a vast enclosure of the lower land. It was six and seven feet high and two feet thick. In parts it ran across turf where no stones were available for building, and in other places it had been built with jigsaw artistry over masses of glacial debris. It would cost more to build such a wall than to buy and stock the farm. On either hand it vanished into the mist, as if bent on a secret errand.

No one today works such long hours as the builders of that and similar walls of the period. W. A. J. Prevost said recently:

> Repairing or building a stone dyke needs little organization and with some encouragement there are surely men who would learn to dyke and to be rewarded by the satisfaction of following a worthwhile and creative occupation. They will not be asked to emulate the deeds and rigours of these warriors who built the first of our hill dykes.

These were built during the summer months when whole families would migrate to the moors with tents, food and the minimum of equipment to do the work. Stones were gathered and rock was quarried and hauled to the site, or carried on hand barrows across ground impassable to horses. Preparations for the erection of park dykes were carried on during the winter months when stones were hauled on the farmer's stone-carts and dumped conveniently, to lie till spring or the coming of warmer weather. Both male and female, old and young, worked at the dyking. The young boys were given the job of *packing* and the women laboured for the men. Georgie Boyes related how he had heard the story of his grandmother 'throwing down stones' to his grandfather some 90 or 100 years ago.

3

TOOLS

One of the major attractions of dry stone walling is its simplicity. The builder pits his wits against the site, using only the actual building material and the very minimum of equipment. No noisy engine, no conveyor belt accompanies his work. The earth's products are being used to confine the earth's livestock, to baffle the winds that would otherwise sweep over them, or to provide shelter and backcloth to a beautiful garden.

Nevertheless any tools used *must* be of high quality. We are dealing with a substance that does not admit to weakness, and a loose hammer shaft or a poor crow-bar can cause a painful accident. All concerned must be familiar with any tools that are used, partly to prevent them from becoming lost. To this end, bright-coloured shafts are an advantage. Yellow- or orange-marked shafts contrast with the greys and browns of stone, and so are less liable to be mislaid or tripped over.

Essential Tools

Walling hammers vary in weight from 1 lb (450 g) to the larger sledge hammer. When dealing with flat, thin, flaky stone as in the Cotswolds, a hammer with one sharp end is an asset.

Hammer heads tend to wear more at the front than at the rear corners when used regularly for walling. For this reason the head may be reversed to ensure more even wear. A large staple is better than a wedge for holding the head in place, as it can easily be tapped out by using a punch. If the head becomes loose through drying out, soak it in a pot of water each night after using.

The traditional 4 lb (1.8 kg) wallers' hammer is not easy to buy. Whatever sort is chosen, the cast iron hammer or mell must never be used on stone, as it is softer than the material being worked, and may cause an accident through splintering.

A walling hammer.

A hammer shaft should be oval rather than round in cross section, to prevent it twisting in the hand. Nor should the shank be too short, or it will have to be gripped awkwardly and too near the head. The waller wishing to fit his own shaft, as many do, will find that ash is best. When cut to the correct length, it should be split rather than sawn to shape.

Another essential tool is the heavy duty garden spade, or possibly the steel shovel. This is needed when a new wall is being built, or when foundations require renovating. Its chief use is in the preparation of foundations, but it also comes into play for tidying an existing wall around the base, or for sheering off a bank in front of which a retaining wall is being built.

Useful Extras

A pick is often useful. If a few more stones are needed for a field wall where stones abound, they may be simply picked up from the surface by putting the pick under one end. Foundation stones that have settled fast may need to be prised up with the pick to release them.

One or two crow-bars are an asset, and they rarely need to be very heavy. Remember that on many walls the tools have to be carried to the job, and carried home again afterwards, so it is a distinct advantage to keep their number and weight to the minimum.

A simple 1 yard or 1 metre steel measure that springs back into its small container is among the waller's friends. It comes in handy for new foundations, for measuring the height and width of the through courses. Skilled workers judge most things by eye, but the beginner is advised to measure.

The same applies to a spirit measure. This is a help in keeping courses running correctly, and for setting lines between frames. When working along a gradient it is particularly easy to leave the horizontal, so check courses by fixing the spirit level to a straight-edged board 3-4 feet (90-120 cm) long.

Buckets, barrows, sledges and trailers are all used by professional wallers for moving stone and a hand barrow, which is simply a trough-like box on long handles, plays its part when two men are available to move stone.

Fine twine, preferably nylon, is needed for guidelines. Nylon does not stretch or rot, and is used between the existing section of wall and the guide frame. It is secured to the wall by metal pins, and these, again, should be brightly painted, for they are easily lost.

Walling Frames

Walling frames are also known as batter frames, wall gauges, patterns or templates. They are simply light timber frames nailed together, and should be made before work starts. Once the specifications of the wall are known, a batter frame is built to correspond with them.

These frames are unnecessary when gapping. For longer lengths they are a definite aid to the beginner, their function being to provide a fast end for the guide lines whose other ends are secured to the completed section.

A plumb line from the top cross-bar helps find the perpendicular. Two frames may occasionally be needed, for example, when stones for the head arrive later or the head is to be built afterwards with masonry. Such an eventuality is so rare that it really need not be anticipated.

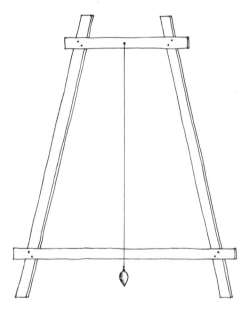

A walling frame. A simple wooden frame of the same dimensions as the wall. Strings are attached either side and re-tied as the wall rises. The other ends of the strings are pinned into the newly built wall and the frame is simply propped in position by a few big stones.

When setting up the wall frame, rest the feet across the foundations at ground level, with the centre line over the centre of the trench. Then check the plumb line, and also ensure that the frame is upright when viewed side on. It is kept in position by a few hefty stones.

Metal pins or wooden splints are then tied to the line ends, and the lines wrapped twice round the legs and secured by pushing the splints or pins down the back. The initial height is one foot from ground level. Be sure to take the lines around the *outside* of the frame, as that is the width required.

If a second frame is used, do the same. More often, the lines will be attached to pins in the existing wall set at the required 1 foot (30 cm) above the ground. Make sure the lines are taut.

When a long stretch is being attempted, it may be the best policy to build up the wall to the height of the line about halfway along its length. Wrap a rag or bunch of grass around the line to prevent chafing, and anchor it at that point.

Protective Gloves

The use of gloves is debatable. The best professional wallers tend to restrict their use to taking down the wall, in itself a fairly precise task (see page 37). They claim that it is impossible to get the correct 'feel' of the stone through gloves. Their hands have of course become toughened through constant contact, and a novice with soft hands might suffer unduly without some protection.

If the use of gloves means the difference between walling and not walling, by all means use them. In the case of a profession where a soft touch is vital — typist, surgeon, pianist — the would-be waller could be deterred for fear of damaging sensitive fingers, and this would be a pity. For such professions, walling is an ideal hobby with considerable therapeutic properties.

The most sensible plan is for each individual to try, with and without gloves. An ordinary household pair suffices. They will not last for very long under constant work, but they are cheap, and thin and pliable enough to gain some feel for the stone through them. Thick, heavy gloves wear much longer, but rob the builder of all contact with the stone.

Windbreaks

Dry stone walling is one of the most enjoyable jobs in the world when the sun shines, breezes are soft and all the birds and animals within sight are contented and happy. Then the work goes with a swing, free from heavy clothing, and each stone warmed by the summer air. Such conditions seldom obtain, and when they do, the farmer or gardener, having other tasks to fulfil, may lack the time for walling. More probably, a length of wall must be built before a particular date, or a gap repaired immediately, whatever the weather.

It is therefore advisable to be prepared. Wind is the chief enemy, and one especially likely to strike on the uplands. A simple windbreak such as a wattle hurdle or even a sheet of galvanized corrugated iron is better than nothing. Poles driven into the ground two yards to windward of the working face suffice to keep the windbreak in place.

For bigger jobs, a purpose-built shelter must be considered. It may be possible to share the capital cost among three or four neighbours, though on the larger farms walling tends to take place at the same time. The usual season is after the ravages of winter and just before lambing in April. As with haymaking equipment, joint ownership is then impractical.

The shelter illustrated is ideal. Its cost was £150 in 1977, and should still be made for under £200. Its designer is Eric Boyes, who contracts all dyking on Buccleuch Estates Ltd., Dumfriesshire. During the desperately severe winter of 1979, only 3½ working days were lost through using the shelter. In the open, work would have been out of the question for days on end.

Constructing a Windbreak

The shelter is light, stable and easily portable. Made from round-section pipes covered by canvas sheets, it is quickly dismantled to fit inside a Land Rover. When in place, two men can move it readily to the next section. Though waterproof, it also allows sufficient light through for working.

Three large canvas sheets are used. One is the main sheet, while the others cover the ends. The canvas must not only be waterproof but thin enough to allow light to shine through. Plastic sheeting is cheaper, but is unsuitable as it tears in high wind.

The sheets withstand three or four years of constant use. Then the

Photo: Audrey Hart

The waller's shelter designed by Eric Boyes. Picture shows the complete shelter erected by Eric Boyes (right) and the author Edward Hart.

The easily erected framework of the shelter. The metal tubes are detachable and the whole thing packs away easily inside a Land Rover. Note canvas cover on ground ready for passing over the frame.

Photo: Audrey Hart

main sheet may be cut in two as it wears, and used for the ends. Often it is practical to have only one end sheeted. Conditions under the cover are unexpectedly comfortable; there is no feeling of claustrophobia or lack of working space.

The frame consists of four arched top pieces which fit into eight side pieces. There are two upper and two lower pieces on each side (see picture). The joints are clearly shown, and are formed on the pipes by welding a section of large-diameter pipe onto one end of the join.

Suitable material is 1 inch (2.5 cm) galvanized iron water pipe, with 1½ inch (4 cm) pipe along the foot. If second-hand aluminium or stainless steel pipe is available, that is quite suitable, but generally much dearer.

To tie down the canvas, loops of flat steel strip are welded onto the bottom pipes. To fix down the shelter, six iron pins are carried, and these may also be used to lever up the frame when setting on a slope. Pins are 3 feet (1 metre) in length, and have a cup-like attachment welded on the top. When extra height is required for levelling purposes the bottom of the frame can be fitted into these cup-like attachments.

The frame width at the base is 13 feet (4 metres), but no cross-pipes are used. Thus sufficient flexibility is gained to settle the frame onto uneven ground or to slightly varying widths. Total length of the shelter is 21½ feet (6½ metres), and height to roof arches 6½ feet (2 metres).

One lesson learnt in practice is always to cover one end. Otherwise a wind tunnel effect is produced, but normally the end to leeward can be left open during working hours. It should be covered at nights, however, otherwise the shelter may fill with snow.

Keeping the main sheet tight at all times helps hold the frame together. Adjustment is by means of guy ropes from the sewn-on canvas loops to the steel loops on the bottom pipes. Stones are used where needed to hold down the end sheets.

Using this shelter, the only weather likely to make walling impossible is hard-driving snow. The shelter protects stone against quite severe frosts, and enables work to proceed in conditions that would be quite unthinkable without its aid.

4

BUILDING THE WALL

Building a dry stone wall is basically a simple job. It is well within the capabilities of any person able to lift one stone on top of another. No skill with tools is needed, for the art of stone walling is to *choose* stones to fit, not *cut* them to fit.

The majority of walls are double walls. They have two sides each built independently, but joined at each course by filling or hearting stones.

The Principles of Walling

The first principle is to build according to the type of wall in your own district. The style of building is evolved by trial and error to find the method most suitable for the class of stone found locally. In Caithness, for example, many walls are flagstones set on edge, and the rest are built from the waste that remains after quarrying the flagstones.

Secondly, a wall must be brought up evenly. It is wrong to build one side up and then the other, finishing the centre later. This rule applies even when two wallers work together; they are a team, not competitors each trying to build higher and faster than the other. A burst is a sure result of uneven building.

The third principle is to prepare all the time for the next move. Starting with a level bottom or footing, it is not too difficult to lay square stones on it to cover the base snugly. But what about the next course or layer? Tops as well as bottoms must be reasonably level, and this is known as level-bed dyking.

Principle number four is 'the less hammering the better'. Eric Boyes, his father and grandfather were all wallers in the Liddesdale district of the Scottish Borders. He says: 'I have known my father and me set down our hammers at the end of a length of wall we were building of a

LIBRARY MAIL

ADDRESS SERVICE REQUESTED

TO:

Hartness Library
Interlibrary Loan
Vermont Technical College
1 Main Street
Randolph Center, VT 05061

MAY BE OPENED FOR POSTAL INSPECTION IF NECESSARY

_____ PARCEL POST	_____ EXPRESS COLLECT
_____ PREINSURED	_____ EXPRESS PREPAID
$ _____ VALUE	

DEMCO

morning, and not pick them up again until we had finished at night. The main use for the hammer is to tap home the copes.'

Time is lost picking up the hammer. If a wall falls down after standing a hundred years, it can be made to stand again for another century, using the same stones in the same shape. It is bad practice to cut a big stone in two to fill a small space; that stone might be needed for a large space later.

Fifthly, use the bigger packing stones lower down. The top two feet of a wall rarely tip over. Leaning starts from the bottom, usually because the foundations themselves begin to tip to one side. All walls settle down and sink into the soil to some extent; the waller's job is to ensure that this settling occurs evenly. Large pieces of packing (hearting) at the base help to strengthen that vital part.

Other commonsense precautions are to ensure freedom from soil or mortar rubble. Soil becomes wet, swells and then splits with the first hard frost, weakening the wall.

Sixthly, look after the middle and the outside will look after itself. This is the exact opposite to what is generally done by untutored amateurs, who naturally like the outside to look smart yet disregard the middle because it is out of sight.

Build two on one and one on two, as does a bricklayer.

The Order of Building
1. Take down the gap, in the case of an existing wall.
2. Prepare foundations.
3. Lay foundations.
4. Build first course.
5. Lay throughbands.
6. Build second course.
7. Lay coverbands.
8. Cope the dyke.
9. Wedge and pin the cope.
10. Clean up stones.

The question of taking down and building the cheek or end is dealt with on page 37.

Although, as mentioned earlier, a professional waller expects to build in one day one rood or 6½ yards (6 metres), Eric Boyes and his father frequently achieved twenty yards between them in the day,

A new Northumbrian roadside wall. The hearting or filling is clearly shown (top of wall in foreground).

which highlights the chief difference of speed between top-class and average. Here we are not concerned with speed. A durable job is our aim, and the person erecting a sheep pen or garden wall is certainly more concerned with appearance and durability than speed.

At least one ton of stone goes into each yard of wall. If the wall has to be taken down first and then rebuilt, that entails handling some 14 tons of stone in the day's work. Therefore it is essential to ease the lifting by taking care in laying out the stone.

Taking Down a Wall

This must be borne in mind when taking down a wall. No stones should be laid nearer than a foot (30 cm) from the wall base, otherwise they impede operations.

1. Lay the coping stones well back. They are first off the wall, and last on. As big rounded stones they have been specially chosen, and must not be used to fill a hole lower down.

2. Lay the coverbands against the copes. These are flat stones 14 inches (35.5 cm) or more ìn length.

3. Lay the throughbands well back.

4. Clean smaller stones away from the wall, evenly on both sides. Leave any standing parts of the wall till last.

5. Take the remaining wall down, making sure that the big foundation stones are close at hand as they are used first.

The foundation is sunk into the ground. When re-making a wall, the decision must be taken as to whether to start again or to build on existing foundation stones. If the foundation is sound, and level, there is no point at all in removing it. If the base has sunk unevenly and tipped, that is where the trouble started, and it *must* be rebuilt. Eric Boyes' father once applied for a dyking contract, and was asked by the farmer whether he would remove the foundations. 'If I need to' was his reply. 'You've got the job', replied the farmer. 'One man said he would always remove them, another said "Never". You are honest.'

A dry stone wall is not like a cement wall, which may be 18 inches (46 cm) wide from bottom to top. The stone wall rests on foundations 28-30 inches (71-76 cm) and culminates at 14 inches (35.5 cm) wide at the top.

If a wall is being rebuilt or a gap mended, the existing line is usually correct. If a new wall is contemplated, its site should be mapped out

Photo: Audrey Hart

Rebuilding a gap. Weak portions must be pulled down in orderly manner to facilitate choice of stones when rebuilding. The smaller hearting stones are clearly seen.

Use of strings inspected by the author on a Dumfriesshire wall.

beforehand. Then, in either case, strings are put on at the correct width a foot above ground level.

Laying the Foundations

Always start at the bottom of a slope. It is quite impossible to con-tinually bend downhill, and steep places can be walled quite success-fully by starting at the foot. People sometimes ask how stone was led up an abrupt incline. The answer is that it was not. It was quarried above, or alongside, and led down. A surprising quantity of stone comes out of quite a small hole.

Unless the original foundation stones are to be retained as already discussed, turf and top soil must be removed to uncover as firm a sub-soil as possible. The shallow trench thus formed must have a level bottom, the first stage in thinking ahead to the next move. The depth of trench varies from about 1½ inches (4 cm) of turf on really stony ground to 6 inches (15 cm) in softer conditions.

Your largest stones are now laid flat and well out to the string. On no account have any parts inside the string, but it matters little if the planned width is exceeded. A scarcement (see Glossary) or overlap of 2 inches (5 cm) either side is allowed. If the wall is being built across a slope, this scarcement should be 4 inches (10 cm) on the downhill or lower side, and little or nothing on the higher.

Although the flattest and best-shaped stones available are used for foundations, some spaces will be left in the centre. These are now packed with stones as big as possible, left slightly higher than the outsides. That is to prepare for the next course, in which stones will slope very slightly outwards to shed the rain. Centre packing is laid, not tamped, a principle that extends the height of the wall. If, on removing the coverbands, daylight can be seen at the foot of the wall, then the middle has been too slackly filled.

The First Course

Having laid the foundations well and truly, the next stage is the first course.

1. Build the stones face outwards and flat, with the nicest and squarest face outermost. The tail (see Glossary) or end facing inwards should be set slightly higher than the face, to help shed water.

2. Break the joints well: build one stone where two join, and two

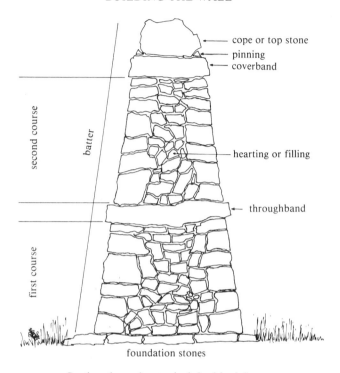

cope or top stone
pinning
coverband

second course

batter

hearting or filling

throughband

first course

foundation stones

Section through a typical double dyke.

stones meeting on the one below them, as does a bricklayer. A 'straight joint', or definite line running straight up, is fatal to any wall.

3. Build side by side. Do not become carried away by building one side up first just because the stones happen to be there. Keep the dyke level.

4. Cut in a little on each course. The waller's term 'cutting in' (see Glossary) refers to the act of building each course slightly in from the one below it. The object is a wall wider at the base than the top, and the amount 'cut in' on each course is traditionally wide enough to allow a mouse to creep along. A finger width is a good guide.

5. Keep the middle full all the time. Do not build two courses of outsides and then decide it was time the gap in the centre received some attention. Fill in, using as large stones as possible, as the work proceeds.

6. At the appropriate and pre-determined height, level the dyke ready for the throughbands. This is where the 1 yard or 1 metre steel rule comes in. Although the hearting has been kept slightly raised ever since the foundations, it must now be set level with the outsides, otherwise the throughbands will rock. Standard height to the first throughbands is 21 inches (53 cm) above ground level.

7. The strings are raised as work progresses, and as the through-bands are approached, strings should be set level with their required position.

Photo: Audrey Hart

Laying the throughbands, a yard apart. Although of irregular shape all reach the full width. The guide strings are being raised and pinned into position for the next course.

This wall collapsed through bad workmanship. There are no throughstones and mortar did not save it. Note the 'buck-and-doe' or 'cock-and-hen' coping stones, which are believed by some wallers to deter stock because of their unsafe appearance.

Laying the Throughbands

1. Throughbands have no value if set too low in the wall. They are there to hold together the two sides.

2. Throughbands *must* reach from side to side. Half-stones, which meet in the middle, are admittedly better than nothing, but every effort should be made to procure a supply of suitable throughbands.

3. Do not have throughbands projecting too far — more than an inch or two — otherwise cattle use them as rubbing posts, and thereby loosen the wall.

4. If building a sheep pen, do not set the throughbands so low that they will catch a sheep on its face, eye or horn. In fact, throughbands built flush with the inside are preferred wherever sheep are tightly penned.

5. If building across a slope, set the wedge side of the throughband to the top side. Then if the projecting throughband is knocked, it tightens itself into the wall. If the wide side of the wedge were at the low side, it could easily drop out.

Building the Second Course

We have now arrived at the second series of courses, which join the throughbands to the coverbands.

1. Set the strings to their new height. Try not to move the string while working; put your hand behind it, and it should not be in the way. A professional waller usually uses string, and may be asked, 'If you're so good, why not go by eye?' The answer is that a very high standard is expected of professionals, and the strings aid perfection.

2. Remember to 'cut' inside the wall width *below* the throughbands. There is always a temptation to cut only from these bands and not from the line of wall below. Expert dykers admit that the throughbands are 'the hardest to get away from'.

3. Start building as before, keeping the middle full.

4. Build the stones side by side, keeping the dyke level.

5. As the wall narrows to fourteen inches (35.5 cm), gradually use smaller stones. The bigger ones should have been built into the lower parts anyway.

6. Build level to the strings, or a little higher on the underside if building across a slope. Up to one inch (2.5 cm) may be allowed, if the slope is steep. On the top course of this section, build the middle level.

You are preparing for the coverbands; remember that they need a flat base.

Working with a hand on either side of the string, the waller keeps his thigh in close contact with the wall, and positions himself so that the exact line is followed.

Laying the Coverbands

Coverbands are stones laid flat on top of the double dyke, projecting about two inches either side. Cope or coping stones are set at right angles to the coverbands, i.e. upright on their edges.

The selection and laying of the cover and cope is the crowning point of all your wall. Coverbands are used in Scotland, but not always elsewhere. Their advocates stress their dual virtues; they bind the wall together again — it has been built in two faces since the throughbands — and they keep rainwater from driving straight down into the wall centre. To build them:

1. Lay coverbands side by side, solid and flat.

2. Set them well out over the double dyke. Knit them to lock one with another, all the time planning the next move, which means laying them as a base for the cope.

Setting the Cope

1. Set the strings along the desired line of the crown. Every cope should touch the string. Coverbands will not be all the same height, so vary copes accordingly, selecting bigger ones where the coverbands are low.

2. Pack the copes closely together. Try to pick the right stone for this crown of the dyke.

3. Wedge the cope, by hitting wedges in at any loose points. Parts of the cope may need no wedges. Use only hard stone, not soft sandstone or the like, and do not leave newly-broken white edges showing. This is where the correct type of hammer is a great aid.

A practical innovation is the use of cement coverbands. These are used by some county councils, and leave a neat and workman-like finish. They have the advantage of standard width and thickness, so provided the wall is brought up properly, they form a level base for the final row of coping stones.

The purist may dislike them. In a garden they are probably best avoided, but it is a question of taste. By all means use them if it means the difference between doing the job with your own hands or bringing in a contractor. The buff-coloured cements now available look less raw, and in some areas there is a distinct difficulty in finding coverbands of the correct dimensions.

The finishing touch. Placing coping stones atop a completed wall.

Section through a new wall in Northumberland. A throughstone shows clearly about halfway up the wall.

Pinning

1. Small bits of spare stone are used to pin the wall. This is more ornamental than anything else, but they give a pleasing finish. Use hard pieces, and keep the weathered side outermost. The white of newly-broken stone spoils the appearance of natural stone.

2. These little wedges are pushed home with the fingers, *never* hammered in. Hammering lifts the copes and generally displaces the firm, sound wall built with such care.

3. Pick the stone to fit the hole. Do not attempt to force a round wedge into a triangular hole.

Cleaning Up

There should not be many stones left, especially in the case of a repair or rebuilding operation. If there are, something has gone wrong. But in any event the ground alongside the wall must be left neat and tidy. A good workman does not leave little bits of stone all over the place, even though they will soon be trodden in by sheep and cattle.

5
GATES AND STILES

Although a dry stone wall may be climbed, the practice is better avoided. If a hundred men clamber over the wall at one point, we may be sure that some stones will be dislodged. Obviously it is necessary to have means of access for stock and vehicles, but these are often fewer than the access needed by walkers.

Gate crooks were once set directly into the stone gate post. These posts were massive affairs. Long, roughly rectangular slabs were quarried and hauled to the site, a hole dug, and the huge rock inserted. Gate 'crooks' — the L-shaped irons supporting the hinges — were secured by chiselling out a hole, inserting the crook, and then filling the space with molten lead. When this lead set, the crook was indeed secure. I have seen gate-posts broken off at this point, the lead remaining immovably fast while the stone gave way. The correct points for the crooks had to be assessed, and the lead poured in while the slab was horizontal.

Cement is nothing like strong enough to hold a crook for a heavy gate. The usual procedure nowadays is to set wooden gate-posts abutting the wall end. Perpendicular finishes are planned with this in mind.

Other means of making access sufficient for a vehicle include stone posts with holes drilled through them, into which long poles are inserted, and pulled out as desired. To make such holes in even a narrow post takes much time and skill, and the technique is one to be admired rather than copied by the novice.

Steps and Stiles
Of the many ways of making a human crossing place, a series of steps is the simplest. This is an ascending line of throughstones long

Eric Boyes (left) and the author completing a cheek or coin end.
Specially selected large square-cornered stones are used for this job.

A cheek; though one in need of a little attention.

A typical style. The gatepost has been cemented, but the facing side shows need for rebuilding. The steps should be embodied more securely.

The simplest form of stile — a massive stone set at a wall corner in Yorkshire.

and level enough to afford secure foothold on either side of the wall. Ideally, each step passes right through the wall, forming a step on the opposite face. At the top there may be a couple of long stakes to afford surer grip, but generally the steps lead up to the coping stones, then down again on the other side. Their main drawback is that they may not be seen by the uninitiated, who will climb needlessly over less suitable places.

A stile must not have too many steps too close together, or crafty hill ewes will learn to negotiate it. It must be built securely, otherwise it will weaken the whole structure. The points to bear in mind when making these very worthwhile features of the countryside are:

1. The first step must not be too low. 18 inches (45 cm) is about right, depending on the slope at the side.

2. The top step should not be more than 2 feet (61 cm) below the top of the wall. Other steps are placed as necessary for comfort.

3. Select your steps before building any into the wall. The biggest and largest are used at the bottom, grading to the top with the smallest.

4. A step thickness of 3-4 inches (7.5-10 cm) is ideal. Projections on either side should be 12-15 inches (30-38 cm). Very long projections are undesirable; they may hurt a galloping beast.

5. An ideal stone is one large enough to project right through both sides of the wall, forming a step either side. If the step is to project on one side only, it should go twice as far into the wall as it projects.

6. Choose stones with firm, flat upper surface. On no account use a convex, slippery step.

7. Anchor the steps with good face stones. They should be twice as long as the step is wide if possible.

Smouts

To make a gateway or opening of any type in a completed wall is a time-consuming and expensive process. It is far better to make any such entrances while the wall is being built. Ways are needed to allow rabbits, water, sheep, or cattle through. All, except the cattle passes, are built low down in the wall, and are variously known as smouts, smoots, hogg holes, thirl holes, lunkie holes, sheep runs or sheep creeps. There are also water gates and cripple holes.

Small smout holes for rabbits or water are but 6 inches (15 cm) or so square. The foundations where the smout crosses the wall should be set

Photo: *Major W. A. J. Prevost*

'The man who built that knew how to build a lunkie.' So said Geordie Boyes about this example of the waller's art. (A lunkie is a passage way through a stone dyke for sheep.)

in the usual way, and care should be taken to ensure they don't rise above ground level. Then the sides are built up as miniature wall heads. Just one or two good stones on either side suffice, but they are important to prevent the hearting being squandered. Then flat lintels (stone slates are ideal) are used to support the rest of the wall. Smouts must never be left simply by omitting a few stones in the wall foot; disaster is sure to follow.

Larger cripple holes and sheep smouts are built on the same principles. Their size often depends on the lintels available. Floorings are important, for quite a large flock may pass in file through the small hole. Thus it is worth taking the trouble to flag the floor.

Water gates require special care. The smout must be built high enough for the lintel to be above any conceivable flood, and foundations and faces must be solid and smooth enough to prevent them being washed out.

Another simple crossing is simply a slit, wide enough for a man's legs but too narrow for a sheep. Such stiles often have a solid stone base some eighteen inches high, to deter the sheep still further. One drawback is that, though they bar a mature ewe, her offspring will slip through until they are several months old. The two faces of the stile reach only to about thigh height, so that the torso moves freely.

Small swinging gates — 'kissing gates' — may be set into the wall, and so baffled that they allow a person to pass halfway through the gap before closing the gate and gaining the other side.

Stone Grouse Butts

A fascinating and specialized example of stone craftsmanship is seen on heather moors. The grouse butt is a protection for guns in the grouse shooting season, and is usually made by moor keepers.

The grouse butt — called a battery in the late nineteenth century — is often made of stone topped with turf. Outside it is camouflaged, inside it is smooth and fitted with niches and shelves for cartridges and lunch bags. Usually about chest high, it is so constructed as to fit in with the surrounding heather, and a whole line of butts may stretch across some declivity showing clearly the contours of the landscape.

Sometimes a butt is half-sunk into the moor; sometimes it is square and sometimes circular. It becomes home to the sportsman, who may ask to be allotted the same one each August. Eric Parker spoke of one such structure: 'It is half-sunk, and you get from it an almost circular view of short heather—heather which ends with a rim of flowers against the sky; and as I see it the sunshine pours down all round it. Bees drone in the bloom, and along the rim, with its tiny pink flowers, hares canter like cats.'

So notice the countryman's craftsmanship; how he paved the floor in a muddy hollow, how cunningly the shelves are fitted, how the natural stone fits into the landscape whence it came, and how the butts themselves became a part of that countryside.

6

RETAINING WALLS

Many gardens and yards benefit from retaining walls. They differ from free-standing walls in that one side holds back soil or loose rock, and this prevents it from squandering across wide areas, sometimes in dangerous manner.

Retaining walls are built to retain and stabilize terraces, road or path cuttings, river banks and other places prone to soil slump or rock slide. It is a mistake to think that a retaining wall can be built in any way you choose just because one side of it rests against something solid. The same basic principles are used in its construction as in free-standing walls. It is made of horizontal courses of face stones with straight batter and small stones.

The retaining wall must sit solidly on its own footings, though these may usually be narrower than for a free-standing wall. If the wall is to be only a yard (1 metre) high, a base width of 1½ feet (46 cm) is adequate. However, if a high wall facing unstable clay or loose scree (or subject to traffic vibration) is planned, the wall may have to be wider than normal.

The first step is to prepare the ground. This should be dug back to a vertical face, taking commonsense precautions against dangerous slips, and allowing at least 6 inches (15 cm) more than the proposed base width, to allow working room.

The foundation trench for the footings is then dug down to firm sub-soil or bed-rock. 6 inches (15 cm) is generally deep enough. A retaining wall is usually comparatively short and work is simplified if the two ends are built first. For them, large stones with a flat bed and *two* good faces should be selected. If the wall merges into the bank at either end, building should start from the head, and the final stones keyed into the bank at their sides as well as their back.

A batter frame cannot often be used in this situation. Guide lines between the two ends are a help for a straight wall, however, and should be raised one foot (30 cm) at a time.

Building starts with horizontal courses, using the biggest stones at the bottom, just as with a free-standing wall. Both inner and outer faces are built together, but it does not matter if the inner face is irregular. In fact it is an advantage for long stones to project into the bank and tie into it.

The Cavity

Filling is done as the work proceeds; and the space between the inner face and the bank is also packed with hard, carefully placed material. Some soil will inevitably fall down; this does not matter so long as it is firmly packed down, and not used to displace all the filling.

Throughs are necessary in a retaining wall. This is not always realized, as their outer faces are usually flush with the wall. Their backs should project right into the cavity between wall and bank. Do not break them off if they are a little too long, rather, make holes in the bank to take them, remembering to allow for them settling in the first years. One should not, therefore, bed them onto solid earth or rock.

It is an advantage to use big stones to pack the cavity. If you find a face stone that does not fit where it was originally required, use it to pack the wall cavity.

If the retaining wall is higher than the bank it holds, finish it just like a free-standing, two-faced wall. When the top is level with or below the bank top, it is better with a flat finish. This may be either a coverband, a flat coping, or even a layer of turf; if the aim is to let earth and plants cover the top, no coping may be necessary.

A neat finish is made by shovelling loose pebbles and earth from the bank top to knit it to the inside of the wall.

7

GRAVEL, COBBLES AND SLATE

Gravel walks make good all-weather paths. Gravel usually must be purchased, and when delivered it should be piled in a rounded heap. It should not be sieved. The larger stones run down the sides of the heap, and are raked off to be used for the foundations.

The walk's route must be first marked out, preferably in smooth curves. The top soil is then removed and used elsewhere in the garden. The wide, shallow trench left is filled with coarse rubble, rocky materials and large pieces of gravel to give a firm foundation. This bottom, which is 10-12 inches (25-30 cm) thick, helps prevent weeds and worm casts appearing.

On it the gravel is laid to 6-8 inches (15-20 cm) deep. The walk is then raked smooth, and bigger pebbles sprinkled back into the mass. During this levelling process, a slight rise to the centre is made, allowing an inch (2.5 cm) of rise for every 5 feet (1.5 m) of width.

The next job is rolling. As each section of about 15 feet (4.6 cm) is laid, it should be rolled lengthways and, if it is wide enough rolled crossways. The person rolling should wear flat shoes, for marks left at this stage are not easy to remove. If several rollings can be given after heavy rain, so much the better. Dust from the gravel helps bind the surface, and this is why sieving should be avoided.

Cobbles

Though stone-work adds character to any farm or garden, one can always rely on cobble-stones to lend an authentic touch of period.

Cobble-stones are generally smooth, and rounded at one end at least. Suitable material is washed up by the sea, found in certain river beds, or occurs where it has been left by glacial action. In towns a supply of cobble-stones may sometimes be found when they are being replaced by more fashionable substitutes.

This method of flooring has certain disadvantages that must be faced. More maintenance is required than for well-laid concrete, since the embedding soil always tends to work up, and needs sweeping on occasion. Really severe frost will lift the stones — but this is also true for concrete, which cracks and must then be taken up entirely and relaid. Cobbles settle back into position.

A warning here against setting them under swinging or sliding doors. In the very hard winter of 1979, one of our sliding garage doors became immobilized because it ran above cobbles which had risen and jammed it fast. The answer here is simply to set the stones a little lower down. A groove of concrete could be used, but that is really unnecessary, and would need substantial foundations to prevent a re-occurrence of the trouble.

Icing is a definite hazard. When rain is followed by a sharp frost, the cobbled yard can become almost unnavigable, and dangerous for elderly people. A sprinkling of sand soon remedies the situation, but the sand must be swept up later. At Thirsk, North Yorkshire, the cobbled market square gave rise to complaints in winter, but beyond doubt it made Thirsk one of the most attractive market towns in the country.

On the other hand, cobble-stones are a considerable advantage on a steep slope. England's highest market town, Alston, Cumbria, has a main street that feels like a gradient of one-in-three in places, and these steepest parts are cobbled. Each stone gives an excellent grip, and their hard wearing qualities withstand continuous traffic.

All cobble-stones are hard-wearing. If they were not they would not have been worn into their distinctive shapes, but would have flaked or disintegrated. The variety of colours, especially by the sea shore, is remarkable and adds a further artistic touch.

Laying

The ideal cobble-stone is pear-shaped, and set blunt end uppermost. The site is prepared by excavating to such a depth that the cobbles set on end will be at exactly the right height. A firm foundation is essential. If not there naturally, it must be provided by a layer of broken rubble, topped with finer material into which the stones can be bedded.

Weeds between the cobble-stones are a time-consuming nuisance. They may be largely avoided by excavating to the necessary depth and laying a polythene sheet before setting the stones.

Sand is the best bedding material. Its lack of vegetable matter ensures that it does not lose bulk to the atmosphere, while its very low fertility discourages weed growth. A shallow layer of sand is spread over the base, and the stones nosed down into it one by one.

A section within easy reach is tamped down on completion, and then more sand is spread over the whole, and brushed in with a stiff broom. Filling-in continues to within about half an inch of the top of the stones.

Each cobble is bedded firmly against its neighbour. The desired level of the yard must be determined *before* the stones are set. If the stones are set too high, pour water into the sand base, and tamp down the cobbles, using a wooden beater.

Patterns can be made by using various colours, or by forming a series of interlocking semi-circles. Such permutations are endless, but for most purposes a straightforward cobbled surface is quite satisfactory.

Renovating a Cobbled Yard

If you are lucky enough to acquire a neglected cobbled yard, its renovation is a worthwhile challenge. Sometimes the stones are completely hidden, making their discovery a complete and pleasant surprise. Over the years, neglected cobbles eventually become carpeted with a thick layer of turf.

The best way of removing turf is by hand after heavy rain. Wearing a pair of gardening gloves, pull up a corner of turf and peel the mass away as far as possible. The cobbles thus revealed appear much cleaner than if a spade is used to push off the debris.

Help from an iron chisel, light pick axe or old screwdriver of sufficient proportions may speed the task, but the main point is to remove the mat of fibre cleanly, rather than leaving loose soil that needs another tedious operation to clear it.

Where old cobbles are bedded in soil, as they usually are, periodic weeding is necessary. It is of course possible to use one of the grass-destroying weed killers, or common salt, but for the many who believe that we do not yet know the full story of chemical weed killers, hard work is the alternative. By using a sharp pointed tool, some of the weed-holding soil between the stones may be removed, and replaced with the more sterile sand.

Though cobble-stones make a warm floor for stock to lie on, they are quite unsuitable for places such as calf pens where regular disinfection is necessary. Germs lodge in the crevices, and make the operation futile. Nor do cobbles serve well where a mechanical fork is used for cleaning. Outside, however, they are a joy, and one of the most pleasant animal sounds I know is that of a favourite horse or pony clip-clopping his way back to the stable over a range of cobble stones.

Stone Slates

It is possible to roof with stone slates, which are flat pieces over 3 feet (90 cm) square and perhaps 2 inches (5 cm) thick. The sheer weight of these slates is such that their use as building material cannot be recommended to the novice. A serious accident could quite easily happen if one is not in control of the situation.

Such slates make ideal paving stones on the ground, but are usually expensive. If a supply is available, and is required for an undeniably attractive roof, then professional help should be enlisted.

When stone slates are removed from a roof, they are usually replaced with something lighter these days. Some stone slates taken off a Dumfriesshire farmstead were found to be held in place with sheep bones!

Common Types of Roofing Slates

Two main types of roofing slate are commonly found. One type uses slates of varying sizes on the same roof. The big ones are laid at the bottom, working up to gradually smaller and smaller slates at the top. The Lancastrian Burlington slate is one such.

Welsh slates are attractive. Blue ones come from Port Noric. They are ordered according to the size required, ranging from about 13 × 7 inches (33 × 18 cm) upwards. Other common sizes are 16 × 8 inches, (40 × 20 cm), 16 × 10 inches (40 × 25 cm), 18 × 9 (40 × 25 cm) inches and 20 × 10 inches (50 × 25 cm).

Westmorland green, so often seen in Lakeland, is a very fine slate. It has stood the test of time, whereas others have been known to turn soft after a few years.

In the building trade, the joiner invariably erects the roof timbers while the slater fixes lathes, for only he can set them at the correct distance as work proceeds.

In England, roofs are commonly underdrawn with lathes, while boards are used in Scotland. The joiner fixes the boards, as they present unlimited choice for nailing on the slates.

Felt is always used under a roof today, and covers the lathes or boards. It is put on by the slater.

Holes are made in the slates before laying begins. A sharp-pointed hammer is the oldest and simplest, but a special drilling machine makes a neater hole. With the hammer punch, there is always a tendency to knock off a flake of slate behind the hole.

Lathes are usually $1\frac{1}{2} \times \frac{3}{4}$ inches (4×2 cm), taking a 2 or $2\frac{1}{2}$-inch (50-65 mm) nail. Galvanized nails of $1\frac{1}{4}$ or $1\frac{3}{4}$ inches (30 or 40 mm) are used to secure the slates.

On the completed roof, only about a third of each slate is visible. The rest overlap to prevent rain and wind entering.

8

STONE IN THE GARDEN

Garden walls are of several types. The boundary wall is similar to the farm wall described in chapter four. It has the advantage of taking little space, and in fact may add to the total gardening area if creepers or climbers spreading over it. Clematis, jasmine, honeysuckle, Russian vine and the wonderful variety of climbing roses are all easily grown over such a wall.

Another sort of wall is the terrace or retaining wall. In a flat garden, raised beds add character and another dimension, and are simply mounds of soil kept in place by retaining walls. The plants grow along the outside of the walls, rooting through and gaining moisture and nourishment from the soil beyond.

Building this type of low wall is comparatively easy (see Chapter six). Ensure that the wall slopes slightly backwards, and have each stone tilted so that it is a little higher at the front than the back. Any rain that falls on the surface is then guided towards the soil.

The same general principle of laying a stone over a space should apply, and see that spaces directly behind the stones are filled, otherwise that part will dry out.

Plants for Walls
A firm base is an essential starting point. Then planting may be done as the building proceeds. One way is to turn the plants out of small pots, lay them on their sides, and allow the foliage to hang over the wall. But do not be too liberal with plants; suitable varieties grow apace in these conditions, and cover up the full beauty of the stones themselves. Weeds must be kept down, and autumn leaves tidied away, otherwise some choice plants will become buried.

If the wall is in shade, a few hardy ferns can be worked into it. At the base, purple primulas and the common yellow primrose are charming, while linaria or toadflax flourishes even where there is little or no soil. Do not forget thymes, thrift, phloxes, the stonecrops and lithospermum. They are common but easy to establish. Those preferring to complicate life by trying something new and doubtful can find plenty of choice in gardener's catalogues.

Once the wall is built and the plants established, little is necessary in the way of maintenance other than that required to prevent overcrowding. That is also true of the rock garden. It affords endless pleasure without hard work, and is capable of taking minor alterations and improvements without upsetting the general scheme.

Setting a Rockery

There are many complicated ways of setting up a rock-garden, but we are concerned mainly with the stone. If your garden is perfectly flat, excavating and building artificial banks are necessary, but an old ditch or bank is capable of being transformed into a beautiful rock garden. The most important point is to make the rockery appear as natural as possible. Smooth mounds of soil with pieces of rock projecting evenly all over are invariably an eyesore.

If you remember the rock plants which grow in natural places, like Exmoor, the Yorkshire or Derbyshire dales or the Cairngorms, and copy nature, you cannot go far wrong. By definition rock plants survive in poor soil, but they will thrive better if they have plenty in which to root.

A gentle slope is better than a steep one, and broad, irregular steps and ledges are more effective than a formal plan. Avoid the regular outline. Set stones to bulge out steeply in one place, and fall away almost flat in another. A variety of twists and turns and corners is best for rockeries.

As with the retaining wall, let the stones slope backwards to catch the rain.

The choice of rocks depends largely on the district in which the rockery is built. The purist will specify types and colours, but we are more concerned with making use of materials readily to hand or easily acquired. Local stone is more likely to blend with local earth than is an imported material.

Colour is possible all the year round with a rockery. Plants should be selected with that in mind, allowing for elevation and amounts of shade and sun. Aubretias are a mainstay in spring, Violas, phloxes and catmint are deservedly popular, while muscari or grape hyacinths are readily obtainable. When rock-gardening has developed into a kind of fever, any number of new plants may be tried, but the basic arrangement of natural rock will be as serviceable as when it was first set into the soil.

The Patio
Much in vogue in modern gardens is the patio. The word and the idea come from the Continent, but a tastefully-designed patio can have a peculiarly Anglo-Saxon look if natural stone is used to advantage.

The patio is basically a paved area on which to set a table and chairs, ready for gardeners to recline in the sun and take well-earned ease.

To be practical, a patio is a most useful link between house and garden. It provides a vantage point for surveying one's domain and fitted with boot scraper and brush it enables shoes to be cleaned before re-entering the house. It dries quickly after rain, unlike a lawn, and for that reason provides a ready base for outdoor gardening jobs not directly connected with the soil.

Even the smallest and most unlikely space can be made into a very presentable patio. The basis of paved flags of natural stone, or indeed of cobbles, lends far more character than mass-manufactured cement blocks however tastefully covered. Stone flags can sometimes be acquired.

Alpines are ideal plants for the patio. They can be arranged among the natural stone so that they flower ten months of the year. Other plants suitable for raised troughs are miniature roses which grow about 9 inches (23 cm) high, backed by others of twice the height.

Troughs
A type of wall garden popular with builders of new houses is the trough on top of the wall. A stone wall, usually cemented, is surmounted with slabs on edge to form a continuous trough into which a variety of plants may be placed. Such sites are liable to dry out in the early stages, before ground cover is gained, but they are a striking addition to any garden once they are established. Again, do not let the growth completely obscure the glowing hues of natural stone.

At one time stone drinking troughs and circular pig troughs with a raised centre could be bought at farm sales for a pound or so. However, those days have gone, for these strictly utilitarian but very beautiful creations are now very much in demand.

All make tasteful additions to any garden or farm entrance. Crocks should be placed in the bottom to help drainage, for there is seldom a drain plug, and tapping one is an expert's job. The mason's chisel marks may be clearly visible, adding to the attraction.

If buying, remember transport. There is a dales saying, 'Nimble as a stone pig trough' to describe anyone particularly ungainly, and few objects of their size seem as heavy and clumsy as these thick-bottomed troughs, purpose-built to defeat a sow's strong nose.

Corners are fairly easily knocked off these troughs, so site them away from busy routes or they are likely to be damaged. Such relics of the past can only become more valuable as the years pass.

9

FLORA AND FAUNA

Once he had been to a place Gray (the fox) never forgot it. His height only allowed him a restricted view of the land, and his landmarks were not like ours, such as a distant church on a hill. His signposts were small things — rocks, sheep trods, smoots through the stone walls, and gateways — and his horizon was bounded by a rise in the ground.

Richard Clapham, *Lakeland Gray.*

Although a dry stone wall does not compare with a thick hedge as a wild life retreat, it is invaluable for certain smaller fauna. Insects and spiders find it a welcome habitat, and some nocturnal species find a daytime haven in the crannies.

Limestone walls are good for snails, and for the larvae of the glow-worm, Lampyris noctiluca, which feed on them. A surprising number of reptiles use the walls, and adders find dry places in them for hibernation. It may not be the farmer's or gardener's purpose to attract adders, but there are few sights in nature so fascinating as a nest of adders appearing for the first time in the spring sunshine.

Blue tits and great tits nest in walls, as do house and tree sparrows, pied wagtails, wheatears, spotted flycatchers, nuthatches and redstarts; but none do so on the scale of Britain's smallest seabird, the storm petrel. Uninhabited islands provide it with abandoned dwellings and ruined field systems, and there are colonies of storm petrel in the great broch of Mousa and in the monastic beehive cells of Great Skellig, County Kerry.

The most attractive mammal known to store food in dry stone walls is the red squirrel, but field voles, house mice, rabbits, hares and rats all use them, while stoats and weasels favour them because of the prey they can find there. Richard Clapham in his story of the fox, Lakeland Gray, depicted the walls in winter.

Towards evening the sky grew overcast, and the wind rose. Flakes of snow began to fall, slanting sharply earthwards. Still harder blew the wind, until a blizzard raged, driving the snow before it in a blinding sheet that plastered the walls with white, fantastic patterns, and piled the snow into huge drifts. Gradually the stone walls disappeared except where here and there a few stones showed.

Towards daybreak the wind died and the snow ceased to fall. Down on the moor, where only the tops of the oldest and longest heather could be seen, the grouse sat on the wall tops which had been blown clear by the wind. A blackcock — looking lonely in his sunlit blue-black plumage — preened himself on a rock.

Here is waller Robert Cairns' views on the bond between walls and wildlife.

The dyker is very close to nature of all sorts. He works away quietly without a great deal of movement, and the whaups (curlews), peewits and even the crows take him for granted. Sheep and cattle come every day at a given time to pass a few moments and have a 'stare' at him. Then the wee stock, mice, voles etc., play about in the old dyke (if rebuilding) and bustle about, flitting, to where? I have seen my father digging out a wee mouse in his nest in winter months, or a hedgehog in his sleep, and carrying them back and building a wee recess in the new dyke with a loose door stone so that they could get away easily when the time came for them to wake up. Time was not too precious then. I have seen him carrying a young hare halfway across a field and making a 'clap' for it, to keep it comfortable until the old one found it.

The old dykes are as dry as can be, and are very often blown full of leaves or old grass, and this provides ample warmth for the smaller animals. That is of course if the dyke is on its feet at all. There is no comfort at all if it's down. The wee birds used to perch very near, in fact in among our fingers, when a hawk or weasel made its appearance.

Lichens, Mosses and Ferns

All types of stone wall are particularly important habitats for lichens, mosses and ferns. These plants add their quota of stability to the structure. Thus where a new wall can be built using a proportion of well-mossed stones the permanency of the structure is immediately assumed. In lowland Britain, stone walls give a home to various saxicolous or rock-dwelling plants. Navelwort or wall pennywort (Umbilicus rupestris) is one such, while the rusty-backed fern (Ceterach officinarum) seems to grow only on walls in Britain.

In high rainfall areas such as the Lake District there can be considerable growth on the north side of a dry stone wall. The south side dries out much quicker, and is a less suitable habitat.

Limestone is noted for its rich variety of plant life, and this distinction remains when it is used in walls. Orange lichens of the genus Caloplaca appear, as do a number of common and rare speelworts and ferns.

The smallest lichens grow in a year, the more conspicuous in three, while ferns and lichens in the Mendips are said to take five years to colonize. If the builder takes care to avoid brushing off mosses and lichens, he or she is well rewarded. It must, however, be borne in mind that a mossy stone has probably been on the north side, and the covering may not survive a southern exposure.

Cement is the worst enemy of plant growth. Using it for copings or plugging up holes prevents many plant species from gaining footholds. Cement is far worse in this respect than the lime mortar used in the past.

One can encourage moss and lichens to grow on a new asbestos roof, by painting it with a thin gruel of oatmeal. The plants then have an immediate food supply, and there is no reason why the same treatment on stone should not produce similar results.

Turf along the wall top helps all manner of plants and insects. However, not everywhere is suitable, for a field boundary is better capped with stone to deter stock, and in a garden turf tends to encourage weeds.

There is no difficulty in rooting all kinds of plants in a retaining wall with earth behind (see page 66). The enthusiastic naturalist must not, however, be tempted into filling crevices in a free-standing dry stone wall with soil. The soil is washed into the middle, freezes, and splits. In so doing it dislodges the hard-won equilibrium of stones on either hand. The wall then bulges and finally collapses. I cannot stress enough that *all* the stone in a dry wall *must* be sound and clean. Any attempt to fill in with soft rubble or mortar is doomed.

Sometimes trees and bushes are found growing out of a wall or building which you have taken over. They must be watched carefully. Charming they undoubtedly are, but as the roots grow, cement, stones or even deep rock will be split. I have a small alder growing from a crack halfway up the barn wall. It is already moving a block of dressed stone, and its days must regrettably be numbered.

10
SAFETY AND THE LAW

The craft of dry stone walling should be one of the safest. No machinery is involved, the work is done on solid and fairly level surfaces, and, for the amateur at least, there is no need to press for undue speed. That mishaps occur is due largely to carelessness and neglect of a few basic principles.

Two people usually make a team, but when more are involved, as in a Conservation Corps exercise, the risks are increased. Be very sure that a rolling stone does not fall on a worker lower down, and at all times keep the working area clean and tidy.

Stone walling injuries are of two main types. Damage to trunk and legs may occur through ill-directed force against too heavy a stone, and there is a danger that stones may be dropped on the hands or feet.

Avoiding Body Injuries

1. Avoid bending more than is necessary — work from the downhill side of a slope.

2. Carry as little as possible uphill. Collect stones from higher up, and carry, sledge or roll them down to the wall.

3. Keep the work area as clear as possible, especially of discarded small stones that form an unstable foothold.

4. Keep tools in the same relative places all the time. Do not lay down hammer shafts and spades where people may trip over them. Paint them a bright colour.

5. Work far enough away from other people so as not to get in their way. Be sure at all times that if you drop a stone, it will not hurt anyone else.

6. Do not try to lift or carry stones that are too heavy for you. Stand comfortably with weight equally on both feet when lifting a big stone.

A steady pull from the tractor and another stone is gained.

Place the feet parallel and slightly apart, so that they are under the stone as you lift it. Keep the back as straight as possible, bending from the knees to take the strain on the leg muscles rather than the back. Gradually ease into the job; work up to it like an athlete in training.

7. You may lift a stone, and then find you cannot make the top of the wall with it in one lift. Move one foot back a little, and rest the stone on your forward thigh.

8. A heavy stone should be tilted onto its end or side, straddled, and rolled forward between the legs. A rectangular slab can be 'walked' by pivoting it on alternate corners.

Avoiding Injuries to the Hands, Feet and Face

1. Wear heavy leather boots, preferably with toe caps. Wellingtons will not do unless they have toe caps. Plimsolls and the like are downright dangerous; they slip and afford no protection if a rock falls on the foot.

2. Do not break small stones by holding them in your hand.

3. When using the hammer, strike square to the stone, not at an angle. Try to stand so that the hammer is central to your body, that is, in line with the bridge of your nose. These techniques help prevent chips flying into the eyes.

4. Rocks vary in their tendency to splinter. Do not hesitate to wear goggles when dealing with types that shatter easily.

5. Try to avoid working in high wind or heavy rain without a shelter, or in severe frost (which also alters the properties of the stone).

Ownership and the Law

The laws about wall and field ownership have been established for many years. In the event of a dispute, the best way is *always* to try to find an amicable solution, and to resort to litigation only when all else fails.

Where there is a ditch on one side the wall is presumed to belong to the owner of the field on whose side of the wall there is no ditch. The side of the ditch farthest from the wall is the boundary.

If the exact edge of the ditch cannot be ascertained through neglect or damage, the distance can sometimes be settled by reference to local custom. The usual width allowed in such cases in 4½ feet (1.4 m) from the base of the wall to the far side of the ditch.

Where there is a wall or bank with ditches on both sides, or on neither side, ownership is usually mentioned in the deeds. The wall usually belongs to both parties when it is ditched on both sides. Should the wall be right on the boundary, the dividing line is taken vertically from the boundary line, and in such cases half belongs to one man and half to the other.

When the Enclosures were awarded, the portion to be walled by each party was often set out in maps, and by a small 'T' mark built with its head into the field whose owner was to build and maintain that section of wall. Some enclosure walls have two heads built touching one another, and joined at the top by a coping. These indicate the boundaries of the sections for which adjacent landlords are responsible.

The question of throughstones denoting ownership is a difficult one. Sometimes the side with projecting 'throughs' faces the owner's land, but in other districts the reverse is the case. Garden walls are usually left smooth on the garden side, to give a neat appearance to the frequently-used patch, and roadside walls are almost always left smooth on the side facing the road. This is done irrespective of who owns the wall and who is responsible for its maintenance, the obvious reason being for the sake of appearance, to reduce damage to vehicles and to deter pedestrians from climbing the wall.

If a wall is built on a boundary line and needs strengthening buttresses, these must be built on the owner's side.

Indeterminate Ownership

'Acts of ownership' include rebuilding or maintaining a wall or bank where ownership is not clear in the deeds. Provided no objection has been raised, twenty years of continual use is usually looked on as an 'immemorable custom' conferring rights of ownership. When there are no acts of ownership, and the origin of the wall cannot be determined, the wall belongs to both owners in equal parts.

In the case of a sale the ownership may be determined by Ordnance Survey field lines. It is certainly wise to try to ascertain the actual boundary before purchase, as OS lines merely indicate the centre of the wall, and not necessarily the true legal boundary.

Maintenance and Liability

The owner of a wall is responsible for repairing it, and for clearing the ditch. When a wall belongs to both parties jointly, it is assumed to be divided down the middle, and each party is responsible for maintaining his half.

Should your wall fall on your neighbour's property, you as owner are liable for compensation, except to any things that grow or rest upon the wall by sufferance. When cleaning out a ditch along a wall or bank, the owner must not cut into his neighbour's land and must throw all spoil onto his own land.

One of the most important laws is that each man must fence against his own stock. He need not fence to keep out another man's stock, but he *must* fence to keep his own in. He cannot claim for damages if his cattle stray and injure themselves on another man's wall or fence. If a neighbour's fence is defective, you must still fence to control your own stock, but you must erect the wall or fence on your own land. In the case of a jointly-owned wall, the owner of stock can place the fence on the wall itself, along the boundary line.

Landlord and Tenant

Though the landlord must often provide materials, the maintenance of walls is usually the tenant's obligation. It is important to have this thoroughly thrashed out in the tenancy agreement. When a tenancy starts, the conditions of the walls should be assessed, and at the end, compensation should be paid for improvements and depreciations to the walls. Scottish law and custom, however, often differ from those in England.

In general, the tenant cannot remove walls or fill in ditches without his landlord's consent.

Garden Walls

Laws on garden walls are fairly precise. A neighbour may not attach any creeping, climbing or trained tree to another's wall, nor may he fasten anything to the wall by nails or rootlets. Nor may loose timbers or heavy articles be placed against another man's wall in a way that may damage it.

The owner's consent is assumed if trained trees or creepers have been allowed to grow over the wall with no disturbance for a number of years. The owner is not then responsible, however, for any unavoidable damage to plants when the structure is repaired.

When a wall belongs to both parties jointly, each can build on his own side for support, but has no right to go beyond the boundary line with any portion of his building.

The owner of a wall beside a public footpath or road is responsible for seeing that the structure does not become a nuisance. 'Nuisance' is defined as something that may cause injury, damage or inconvenience to others.

One final and perhaps rather optimistic point of law concerns finding articles of intrinsic, archaeological or historical value in a wall. In England, where this occurs very rarely, the finds may belong to the owner of the land, but the most sensible course is to report any such finds to the police, who can then advise on action.

PROFESSIONAL WALLING, TRAINING AND COMPETITIONS

The object of this book is to interest the keen gardener or small farmer in the beauty, endurance and utility of natural stone. It may be that enthusiasm is so stimulated, and a natural and perhaps unsuspected knack discovered, that the person who has built a few lengths of wall at home seeks further outlets.

There is no reason to be hesitant. If your wall withstands the classic test of the old-timers — standing back, and taking a running jump halfway up the wall with one foot — you can build for other people. By taking a length on contract, that is, working for so much per yard, you have no fears about overcharging while still operating at a fairly low rate of output.

Walling as a Profession

Anyone contemplating walling as a profession, either part-time or full-time, must be prepared to work in bad weather. Even with a shelter conditions are by no means pleasant on many occasions.

Professional wallers seldom lack work. They may have to travel, sometimes far from home, and this angle must be considered. A length of garden wall was recently erected in Northamptonshire, using the local golden stone held together with cement, presumably to prevent it falling down, at the cost of £1,000. Two men from the hill districts could have halved the price and still made a useful profit.

Joining the Dry Stone Walling Association, Gatehouse-of-Fleet, Kirkcudbrightshire, is obviously a good idea. This excellent body informs members of work available. County councils, private gardeners and the growing number of country parks will all need wallers for the foreseeable future. The Dry Stone Walling Association is an organization run entirely by voluntary help — it does its best to

A fine piece of workmanship in West Yorkshire by Walter Newbould and his two sons in 1971. Some very large stones have been built into the base.

Photo: Major W. A. J. Prevost

Professional wallers hard at work. No standing about musing, but constant endeavour resulting in a continuous flow of stones into the correct positions at each move of the hands.

keep dykers and wallers informed of any contract work etc. available, or equally, puts prospective employers in touch with the dykers/ wallers in their area. But the Association is *not* an Employment Agency! Association funds depend mainly on members' annual subscriptions and are used on any project that helps to foster and maintain the craft, encourage training, stage demonstrations etc. Consequently it is vital to enclose with any enquiry sent a stamped, addressed envelope.

Courses

The National Federation of Young Farmers' Clubs give copies of tests and guide notes. The standards are set by the National Proficiency Tests Council, and those who pass the examination are fully qualified to do dry stone walling work.

West Dean College in Chichester conducts five-day courses in walling in flint and stone with mortar.

Northumberland National Farmers Union and Agricultural Training Board have combined in a scheme to attract school leavers into walling. The county NFU acts as employer, with the help of Government funds, and farmers whose walls need repair pay a small sum and supply the necessary stone. There are facilities for selected unemployed persons between ages of 16-18 under the Manpower Services Commission Work Experience Programme.

Vocational Training Grants provide another way in which craftsmen wallers can take on unemployed workers over 18 as trainees. In this case apply to the local Department of Employment.

The Agricultural Training Board, Scottish Regional Office, is especially active in promoting walling courses. Similarly in Cumbria, the ATB's Lakeland Officer organizes courses and other parts of England and Wales may do likewise if demand is sufficient. Another helpful body is CoSIRA, (Council for Small Industries in Rural Areas) and the British Trust for Conservation Volunteers runs training courses. For further details of all of the above see Useful Addresses.

Peebleshire dyker Robert Cairns gives this stern warning to would-be professional wallers:

The dyker on piece work is working at a very high pitch, in fact he has trained himself just as a boxer or athlete would before entering a championship. I can remember when we were off work for a week (bad weather), it took us nearly a fortnight to get our hand in again, and when I had to do some dyking here, after working at other jobs for some time, I couldn't get speed up at all, and I had to work very hard to make a show at all. A great deal of rubbish is spoken about dry dykes and dykers by people who pretend to be interested and who write about it. There is nothing mysterious about it at all. I have heard a lot of masons talking about dykers never laying down a stone once it is lifted. They didn't know I was a dyker of course. The fact is that the dyker has trained his eye and his hand to work together to such a pitch that he simply doesn't lift a stone at all unless it *will* fit either one bed or another. He just can't afford it!

Competitions

An excellent example is set by those agricultural societies that organize dry stone walling competitions. They are a great attraction. Throughout the day wallers work at their own stretch, singly or in pairs according to the nature of the competition, and there is invariably a constant passing of spectators from one to another, comparing, admiring and sometimes learning.

One of the greatest pioneers in reviving stone dyking was the late Colonel Rainsford-Hannay. He recalled:

'In 1938, in the Stewartry of Kirkcudbright, it was felt that something should be done about maintaining this old craft and a committee of landowners and farmers was formed. It was decided to hold a dyking competition and a circular was sent to some eighty people who might be interested. In October 1939, during the "Phoney War", the first competition was held.

The committee selected a dyke 4 feet 4 inches high on one side and 4 feet 2 inches high on the other. To get spectators and entrance money we had to choose a dyke near the main road, where people could be dropped by bus. The competition was open to all and there were twenty-eight entries out of which twenty-six competed. This fairly astonished the pessimists.

Much of the dyke chosen was quite good, but there were a lot of weak places. These places were pulled down level and the gaps measured. After the men had arranged their stones, they started work at a signal. They built to the specification given earlier. Tasks for pairs were 19 feet, and for single workers 9 feet. Time allotted 5½ hours.

There were two classes: one for professional dykers, whether contract workers or men employed on estates and the other included any other dykers (mostly shepherds and farm hands). Only two men in the latter class failed to finish their task in time. The professionals all finished early and their work was uniformly good. The second prize winners in class A finished in 3¼ hours, which works out at over 23 feet per man for an eight-hour day. Actually, they could have finished much sooner had they wanted to.

1940 was far too anxious a time, but in 1941, 1945, 1946, 1949, 1951 and 1953 and 1955 further competitions were held. Owing to the ''call-up'' numbers were fewer, but only once were there less than twenty men competing.

In 1948 a dyking class was held, eight men and the instructor being billeted on neighbouring farms. A second class was held in 1950.

In 1940, I was asked to give a broadcast about stone dykes. On the way up to Edinburgh, the news came out that France had capitulated or at any rate had asked for an armistice. Terrible news! I asked the announcer if the broadcast at 1.15 p.m., after the 1 o'clock News, should not be cancelled. But the announcer would have none of it. ''Good for morale'', he said. Perhaps he was right; who knows? At any rate, after the News, when Europe rocked and seemed to be crashing about our heads, a voice, speaking about the art of building dry stone dykes, broke in upon the ears of a stunned world. Some people did listen, perhaps as a relief from the dire tidings from Europe, and I got quite a fan mail that week. One letter from a man who had served with me began, ''Dear Colonel, Please forward to the above address 100 yards of dry stone dyke, carriage paid''. So one man's morale stayed high.'

Young Farmers' Clubs have taken up the idea, and have organized stone walling competitions, sometimes in conjunction with hedging and ploughing matches. Not every district can achieve this combination, but in the mixed farming areas of the lower dales, where wall and hedge meet and intermingle, and where some cropping takes place, the three crafts make a wonderful competition.

The usual procedure is for each competitor to be allotted a few yards of deteriorating wall. He or she must take down the existing wall and completely rebuild.

GLOSSARY

(A)   Upper Annandale.
(C)   Chambers Scots Dictionary.
(G)   Galloway.
(J)   Jamieson's Dictionary of the Scottish Language.
(M)   MacTaggart's Gallovidian Encyclopedia.
(SND) Scottish National Dictionary.

Band, Band-stone (A). See *Through Band.*
Band Height. The height of a stone-dyke at which it is intended to lay the through bands.
Batter (J). The slope (taper) of a wall or hedge, expressed as an angle or as a ratio of horizontal to vertical dimensions.
Batter frame. A wooden or metal frame used as a guide to the correct batter and to the heights of throughs, topstones etc., when building a wall or hedge. Also known as a pattern (South West), template or wall gauge (Cotswolds) or walling dyke frame (Scotland).
Bed. Deposition layer in sedimentary rock. In walling, the flattish base of a stone or any plane along which it splits readily.
Bee bole. A niche in a wall built to store straw bee skeps.
Breccia. Rock composed of sharp-angled fragments cemented in a fine matrix.
Broch. An Iron Age round tower built of dry stonework as a citadel against raiders. Found especially in the Orkneys and Shetlands.
Buck-and-doe. A form of coping alternating large and small upright topstones. Also known as cock-and-hen (Cotswolds).
Bunkering (A). The use of two small stones instead of one long stone when building the single.
Butt. See *Hudd.*

Capes, Cape-stanes or *Cope Stones* (J). See *Top Stones.*

Chain. A traditional unit of measurement, 22 yards (20 m).

Cheek (A). The end or the beginning of a stone dyke. Hence 'Gate cheeks', or the cheeks of a gateway.

Chip and Block. A type of stone hedging in which small stones (chips) and large stones (blocks) are intermixed within each course (Devon).

Chuckie Stane (J). Stones composed mainly of quartz crystals. The 'White Shell' on Fingland in Tweed was built in 1930 entirely of chuckie stanes by two Moffat dykers. This type of stone is very rough to work with.

Clap Dyke (SND). An earthen dyke or fence 'so called because they were clapped with a spade, to make them solid'.

Clearance Wall. A wall built largely from stones cleared from the surface of adjacent land. When the wall is made extra wide to accommodate the stones it is also known as an accretion wall or consumption dyke (Scotland).

Clevage. The structure by which certain metamorphic rocks, e.g. slate, split most readily, often at an angle to the original bedding plane.

Clonks (G). Big stones in the single, below the cope stones.

Consumption Dyke. Dykes built to 'consume' the stones which were cleared off the land. On the estate of Glassel in Kincardineshire during the last quarter of the eighteenth century 150 Scots acres of unploughable land were improved and the enormous quantities of stone taken off the surface were built into consumption dykes, from 12 to 16 feet thick and many hundreds of yards in length. (W. Alexander. Notes and Sketches, pub. 1877, page 104.) Consumption dykes are found in Aberdeenshire, mostly near Monymusk. The Kingswell Consumption Dyke is 27 feet wide at the top and 5 feet high.

Coping. The line of stones along the top of the wall which protects the structure beneath. Also known as the cap, comb (Cotswold and South West), cope or topping.

Course. A layer of stones in the face of a wall or hedge.

Coverband (G). A layer of throughstones placed on top of the double dyking to anchor it and form a base for the coping (Scotland).

Covers, Cover Stones (A). Flat stones of a minimum specified length which are laid on top of and cover the double.

Cripple Hole. A rectangular opening at the base of a wall built to permit the passage of sheep. Also known as a hogg hole, lonky or lunky hole, smoot sheep run, sheep smoose, smout hole, thawl or thirl hole.

Crown. The top of a bank or hedge. Also known as a comb (Devon).

Cundie (J). A covered opening through or under a stone dyke, made to allow the passage of water.

Cutting the Found (A). Reducing the width of the foundation of a stone-dyke when rebuilding is known as cutting the found. This has the effect of thinning the dyke, a procedure not viewed with favour by conscientious dykers.

Dam Dyke (M). A mound of earth flung across a stream to confine the water, for mechanical reasons.

Ditch. A long narrow trench dug as a boundary, barrier or drain. In Ireland and parts of Wales, a bank or other raised barrier.

Double Dyking (A and G). The part of a normal dry stone wall which has two rows of face stones packed between with fillings. Also known as doubling. Distinguished from single dyking in which only one thickness of stones is used with no fillings.

Dry Stone Wall. A wall built without mortar. Also known as a drystane dyke (Scotland) or dry stone hedge (Cornwall).

Dyke. A wall (Scotland). Also spelt dike.

Elvan. See *Whinstone.*

Face. An exposed side of a wall, hedge or bank.

Face Stone. A stone whose outer surface forms part of the face of the wall.

Fail Dyke, Feal Dyke (J). A wall built of sods.

False Band. See *Through Band.*

Fence. A structure serving as an enclosure, barrier or boundary, loosely used to include walls, hedges, banks, ditches and dykes.

Fillings. Small, irregular stones placed between the two faces of a wall to pack the space between them. Also known as hearting (Scotland).

Fissile. Rock characterized by a tendency to split readily along planes of bedding or cleavage.

Flag. A thin-bedded sandstone which breaks up readily into flat slabs. Loosely used for a flat slab of any type.

Fleet Dyke (J). Embankments erected for the purpose of preventing erosion.

Foliation. The structure, similar to but less regular and perfect than cleavage, by which the minerals in rocks such as schist and gneiss are arranged in parallel planes due to metamorphism.

Footing. A stone at the base of a wall, or the foundation of a wall in general. Also known as a found (J).

Freestone. Stone which has no tendency to split in any particular direction.

Galloway-Dyke. 'A Stone-dyke built 5 feet 3 inches (1.6 m) high and up to 6 feet (1.8 m), and 32 inches (81 cm) at the base. The cover bands are put on at about 40 inches (1 m) above the grass, the usual hearting and packing being carried out, the through bands having been laid at 21 inches (53 cm) above the grass. The next 22 inches (56 cm) and more consist of large rough stones, laid and interlocking towards the level top, but with wide interstices between them, and the light showing through. No pinning is done to this portion.' (Rainsford-Hannay, Trans. Highland Soc., Vol. 56, 1944.)

Galloway Hedge. A combination of a dry stone wall and thorn hedge which is constructed along a hillside so that the hedge shrubs root through the wall and are protected by it from livestock on the uphill side.

Gap. A breach in a wall due to defect or damage. (v) To fall, leaving a breach; to repair a breach.

Grit. Any hard sandstone, especially one in which small pebbles are mixed with the sand to give a rough texture suitable for millstones. Also known as gritstone.

Gull. Gull is an archaic word used by Smith, of Borgue, in his General View of Galloway. Gulls were the stones immediately above the cover bands which were so dressed as to lie solid upon them without being supported by small stones or pinnings.

Half Dyke (A). A stone-dyke built so that the double and single both measure half the total height. Thus a half-and-half dyke is half double and half single.

Hand Barrow. Type of rack on which two men carried heavy stones. It was laid across the dyke, and the stones rolled off into the exact position required.

Head. The smooth, vertical end of a wall or section of wall. Also known as a cheek (Scotland). See *Wall Head.*

Head Dyke (J). A fence or wall dividing the green pasture or arable from the heath or moor.

Hearting (G). See *Packing.*

Hedge. A line of closely planted shrubs or low-growing trees. In Devon, an earth-filled bank used as a barrier or boundary and faced with stones or turf. In Cornwall, any earth or stone barrier.

Herringbone. A type of stone fencing in which alternate courses of stones are angled in opposite directions. Particularly found in Cornwall.

Horse's Head (A). This is the name given to a stone which is round and which will not lie.

Hud, Hudd (C). A part of a stone-dyke built with single stones which go from side to side. Synonymous with Sneck. Snecks are sometimes built by dykers to strengthen the dyke if there are sufficient stones available. A *Butt and Hudd,* according to the late John Broadfoot, of Sanquhar, consists of alternate lengths of stone-dyke built double and single in panels.

Joint. In walling, the crack between two adjacent stones in a course.

Lamination. A structure of fine, closely spaced layering along the bedding planes in certain sedimentary rocks.

Lift (G). See *Scarcement.*

Line, to Line the Dyke (A). The process of using a line of string when finishing the top of a stone-dyke and when laying the cope stones. This ensures a neat finish, a straight top and 'lines the dyke with the ground'.

Lintel. A stone slab or wood or metal beam placed over an opening to bridge it and support the structure above.

Locked Top. A type of coping in which the topstones are pinned into a solid unit using long thin wedge stones. Mainly Scotland.

Lunkie (J). A passage way through a stone-dyke, made for sheep. The 'lunkie-hole' should be made narrower at the bottom than at the middle and top.

March Dyke. A major enclosure wall running between estates (Scotland).

Mash Hammer (J). A mash hammer, weighing from 4½ to 5 lbs (2-2.2 kg), was sometimes used for breaking up stones. The dyker's hammer in everyday use weighs 2½ to 3 lbs (1-1.4 kg) only.

Masonry. Stonework characterized by the use of cut and trimmed stone.

Oolite. Rock, usually limestone, composed of small round calcareous grains.

Packing (A). Inserting or packing stones into the space between the outside stones of the double. This part of the building, called hearting in Galloway, must be done thoroughly. When examining the work on the completion of a newly built dyke, the solidity of the double was tested by kicking. If the stones went in there was not enough packing.

Pein. The striking surface of a hammer head.

Pin, Pinn (J). To wedge and make secure with chips of stone, to fill up with pin stanes or pinnings.

Quartzite. Sandstone consisting mainly of quartz grains cemented into a hard continuous mass by silica.

Reg. Any of several kinds of hard coarse rock, mainly limestones, which break irregularly. Also known as ragstone.

Retaining Wall. A wall built across the face of a bank or slope to keep the soil from slipping.

Rhyolite. A volcanic rock similar in composition to granite and usually exhibiting flow lines.

Rickle (J and M). To pile up in a loose manner. Rickle, when used as a noun, can refer to a badly built stone-dyke.

Rickle-Dyke (J). A wall built firmly at the bottom, but having the top only the thickness of the single stones, loosely piled one above the other. (North of Scotland.)

Risband (A). Stones should be so laid as to overlap one another, to break the joints in order to bind and connect them. If two or more joints are not broken the result is an obvious vertical line of unbroken joints. This line is called a risband or straight joint.

Rood. The traditional unit of wall measurement, 6 yards (5.5 m) in granite districts in Scotland and 7 yards (6.4 m) in limestone districts and through most of Yorkshire.

Rough Skinned (A). A rough skinned stone is one which cannot be broken.

Rubble. Rough, mainly untrimmed, walling stone; walls or copings characterized by such stone.

Runner. A long face stone used in a wall head (Scotland).

Scarcement (J). The in-set between the outer edge of the footings and the first course of face stones (Scotland).

Scuncheon (J), *Sconcheon* (C). See *Cheek.*

Shooting Butt. A small, usually circular enclosure built to shelter grouse shooters.

Single (A). The single, or top courses of single stones, one stone thick, from the cover stones to the coping of a stone-dyke. The Highlander's Wall in Eskdalemuir is built of single large boulders placed one above the other, but single dykes are uncommon. Another example is seen on Roundstonefoot in Moffat parish.

Slap (J and M). A breach in a stone-dyke.

Sled or Sledge. Pony or horse drawn, for carting stone, especially useful on slopes.

Sleek, Sleekit (J). Smooth. Used to describe the double of a stone-dyke which has been built neatly, to please the eye. Such a dyke is said to be 'weel-skinned'.

Smoot. A small rectangular opening in the base of a wall. Rabbit smoots (Scotland: pen hole; Mendips: pop hole) are designed to permit the passage of hares and rabbits. Water smoots (Scotland: double water pen) are designed to permit the passage of water.

Snap Dyke (J). A stone fence, from 4 feet to 6 feet (1.2-1.8 m) in height, strong and firmly locked together at the top.

Sneck (J). See *Hudd.*

Sod Coping, Sod Tops (A). Sods cut from stone-free, tough turf, used to finish a stone-dyke instead of stones. Sods used for this purpose are cut to an exact size. The sods are laid flat as covers to form the top. Two sods make the cover, being laid one on top of the other, with the grass inwards.

Spar. Any of various non-metallic, lustrous and readily cleaved minerals, such as felspar.

Split Bands (A). See *Through Band.*

Stile. A set of steps over, or an opening through, a wall, hedge or other fence designed to allow the passage to pedestrians but not livestock.

Stone Carts. Carts used for hauling stones were specially made for this purpose, with low sides. It is said that three of these cart-loads were required to build one yard of stone-dyke. Another estimate is two farm-carts loads of stones for every yard — one load each side. Two stone carts are included in an inventory of farm implements, made on Craigbeck in Moffat parish in 1827.

Stoop. An upright monolith set into the ground against the wall head of a gate or stile. Also spelled Stoup.

Subdivision Wall. A wall built to divide a major enclosure into smaller sections, often somewhat lower and less well constructed than the boundary wall.

Sunk Dyke (J). A dyke built of stones or sods on the one side, and of earth on the other.

Sunk Fence (G). A combination of dyke and hedge, sometimes called a Galloway Hedge (Rainsford-Hannay).

Taff Dyke (M). A fence made of turf.

Tail. The part of the stone that is fitted away from the wall face.

Thin (A). To thin a dyke. See *Cutting a Found.*

Through, Through Band (M). The long stones which bind dykes, which strengthen and 'tie' the dyke together. Through bands must never be omitted, but it sometimes happens that a Split Band or False Band is used as a makeshift. A split band consists of two stones, laid alongside each other across the centre of the double. The insertion of split bands is a deceitful practice if the dyke is being built to specification at a contract price.

Dykers have been known to use wooden through bands as a substitute for stone, and oak bands were used in the construction of a dyke on Poldean in Wamphray parish. Red cedar, shingles were used as covers in a 100-year-old dyke at Galt in Canada.

Tie. A through used in a wall head (Scotland).

Top (A). To top, to lay the top stones on a dry stone dyke. The stones are set only from the lower end.

Top Stones (A). Stones of certain dimensions and shape selected and used for the coping of a stone dyke. These were sometimes stipulated to be 10 inches (25 cm) or more high.

Tumbling Tom (A). The name given to an instrument used for measuring stone dykes. It consisted of a kind of an adjustable frame, with two arms which dropped down on both sides of the dyke which it was required to measure.

Wedge. A small stone placed under or behind a face stone to position it securely.

Well Skinned. See *Sleekit.*

Whinstone. Any hard dark-coloured rock such as greenstone, basalt, chert or quartzose sandstone. Also known as elvan or elvin (Cornwall).

Wall Head. Definite squared off junction. If it denotes a change of ownership, a 'T' may be engraved.

BIBLIOGRAPHY

Cairns, Robert: *Dry Stone Dyking* (Biggar Museum Trust, 1975).
Clapham, Richard: *Lakeland Gray* (Blandford Press, 1947).
Firbank, Thomas: *I Bought a Mountain* (Harrap, 1940).
Grounds, Roger: *Making and Planning a Small Garden* (Ward Lock, 1973).
Hoskins, W. G.: *History from the Farm* (Faber, 1969).
Lucas Philips, C. E.: *Climbing Plants for Walls and Garden* (Heinemann, 1967).
Rainsford-Hannay, F.: *Dry Stone Walling* (Stewartry Drystane Dyking Committee, 1976).
Raistrick, Arthur: *The Pennine Walls* (Dalesman Publishing Co., Clapham, Lancs., 1946).
Rollinson, William: *Lakeland Walls* (Dalesman Publishing Co., Clapham, Lancashire, 1972).
Symon, J. A.: *Scottish Farming* (Oliver and Boyd, 1959).
Vivian, John: *Building Stone Walls* (Garden Way Publishing, 1976).
Various authors: *Dry Stone Walling* (British Trust for Conservation Volunteers, 1977). Available from BTCV, Zoological Gardens, Regents Park, London NW1 4RY.

USEFUL ADDRESSES

Lakeland Officer, Agricultural Training Board, High Aketon, Waverton, Wigton, Cumbria.

Agricultural Training Board, Scottish Regional Office, 13 Marshall Place, Perth PH2 8AH.

British Trust for Conservation Volunteers, Zoological Gardens, Regents Park, London NW1 4RY.

Cornish Stone Hedging Association, 15 Trewirgie Road, Redruth, Cornwall.

CoSIRA, PO Box 717, 35 Camp Road, Wimbledon Common, London SW1 4UP.

Dry Stone Walling Association, Gatehouse-of-Fleet, Kirkcudbright-shire.

National Farmers Union, Clayton Road, Jesmond, Newcastle-upon-Tyne NE2 1UA.

National Proficiency Tests Council, c/o NFYFC, National Agricultural Centre, Kenilworth, Warwickshire CV8 2LG.

West Dean College, West Dean, Chichester, Sussex PO18 0QZ.

INDEX

accident, avoidance, 73, 75
allotments, 19

batter, 22, 59, 85
batter frames, 28, 60, 85
battery (butt), 57
broch, 21, 85
boundary walls, 9, 66
buttresses, 76

cement, 9, 11, 14, 46, 72, 79
cheek, 35, 86
cleaning up, 49
cobbles, 61
competitions, 83, 84
consumption dyke or clearance
   wall, 14, 21, 86
coping stones, 14, 22, 35, 37, 46,
   60, 86
Cornish stone hedges, 21
Cotswold stone, 11, 25
coverbands, 35, 37, 40, 44, 45,
   46, 60, 86
cripple holes, 57, 86
cutting in, 41

Dry Stone Walling Association,
   79, 94

enclosures, 19

face stones, 55, 87
fauna, 70
ferns, 66, 71, 72
filling (hearting), 34, 35, 41, 57,
   60, 89
flora, 70
foundations, 27, 37, 40, 55, 57

garden stone, 66, 77
gates, 52
gloves, 29
gravel walks, 61
grouse butts, 57, 90

hearting, 34, 35, 41, 57, 60, 89
hogg holes, 55

injury prevention, 73, 75

kissing gates, 57

Lakeland stone, 11
landlord and tenant, 77
land reclamation, 21
law and ownership, 75, 76
laying cobbles, 62
lead, 50
legal liability, 77
level-bed dyking, 34
lichen, 71, 72

lime mortar, 72
limestone, 72
lintel, 57, 89
'livestock damage, 15, 21, 44
lunkie, 55, 89

maintenance, 77
march walls, 9, 89
mosses, 71, 72

overlap, 40

packing (hearting), 34, 35, 41,
     57, 60, 89
patio, 68
paving stones, 64
pinning, 49, 90
principles of walling, 34

retaining walls, 27, 59, 60, 72,
     90
rockery, 67
roofing slates, 64

safety, 73, 75
scarcement, 40, 90
sheep holes or sheep creeps, 55,
     57
shooting butt, 57, 90

slit stile, 57
smoots, 55, 91
smouts, 55, 57
splintering stone, 75
stile, 14, 50, 55, 57, 91
stone slate, 61, 64
stone thieving, 14
swinging gates, 57

taking down walls, 37
terraces, 11, 66
thirl holes, 55
through courses or through
     bands, 27, 41, 44, 50, 60, 76,
     92
timing, 15
tools, 14, 25, 27, 46, 65
traffic damage, 15
training courses, 82
tree damage, 15
turves or tobs, 21

walling as a profession, 79
walling frame, 28
wall-top trough, 68
Wensleydale stone, 11
windbreaks, 30

Young Farmers Club, 18, 82, 84